Hans H. Ørberg

LINGVA LATINA

PER SE ILLVSTRATA

Latin-English Vocabulary

I

LINGVA LATINA
PER SE ILLVSTRATA

Pars I:
Familia Romana (1-58510-201-6; hard cover 1-58510-238-5)
Latine Disco: Student's Manual (1-58510-050-1)
Grammatica Latina (1-58510-223-7)
Exercitia Latina I (1-58510-212-1)
Latin-English Vocabulary (1-58510-049-8)
Lingva Latina: Familia Romana CD-ROM for PC (87-90696-08-5)
Lingva Latina Exercitia Latina I CD-ROM for PC (87-90696-10-7)

Pars II:
Roma Aeterna (87-997016-8-5)
Exercitia Latina II (87-90696-05-0)
Indices (87-997016-9-3)
Instructions for Part II (1-58510-055-2)
Latin-English Vocabulary (1-58510-052-8)
Lingva Latina: Roma Aeterna CD-ROM For PC (87-90696-09-3)
Lingva Latina Exercitia Latina II CD-ROM for PC (87-90696-12-3)

Ancillaries:
Mac OSX CD-ROM for Parts I & II (text, Exercitia, etc) (87-90696-13-1)
Caesaris: Commentarii De Bello Gallico (87-90696-06-9)
Colloqvia Personarvm (1-58510-156-7)
Menaechmi ex Plavti Comoedia (1-58510-051-X)
Petronivs: Cena Trimalchionis (87-90696-04-2)
Plavtus: Amphitryo (87-997016-7-7)
Sallustius & Cicero: Catilina (87-90696-11-5)
Sermones Romani (97-90696-07-7)
Transparency Masters & CD w/ images (Mac/PC) (1-58510-239-3)

For further information on the complete series and new titles, visit www.pullins.com.

ISBN 978-1-58510-049-1
ISBN 10: 1-58510-049-8

Distributed by Focus Publishing / R Pullins Company, PO Box 369, Newburyport, MA 01950 (www.pullins.com) with permission of Domus Latina.

0707TC

Printed in Canada.

A

ā/ab/abs *prp +abl*	from, of, since, by
ab-dūcere	take away, carry off
ab-errāre	wander away, stray
ab-esse ā-fuisse	be absent/away/distant
ab-icere	throw away
ab-īre -eō -iisse	go away
abs *v.* ā/ab/abs	
absēns -entis *adi*	absent
abs-tinēre	keep off
ac *v.* atque/ac	
ac-cēdere	approach, come near
accendere -disse -ēnsum	light, inflame
ac-cidere -disse	happen, occur
ac-cipere	receive
ac-cubāre	recline at table
ac-cumbere -cubuisse	lie down at table
ac-currere -rrisse	come running
accūsāre	accuse
ācer -cris -cre	keen, active, fierce
acerbus -a -um	sour, bitter
aciēs -ēī *f*	line of battle
acūtus -a -um	sharp
ad *prp +acc*	to, toward, by, at, till
ad-dere -didisse -ditum	add
ad-esse af-fuisse (*+dat*)	be present, stand by
ad-hūc	so far, till now, still
ad-icere	add
ad-īre -eō -iisse -itum	go to, approach
ad-iungere	join to, add
ad-iuvāre	help
ad-mīrārī	admire, wonder at
admīrātiō -ōnis *f*	wonder, admiration
ad-mittere	let in, admit
ad-nectere -xuisse -xum	attach, connect
ad-ōrāre	worship, adore
adulēscēns -entis *m*	young man
ad-vehere	carry, convey (to)
ad-venīre	arrive
adversus/-um *prp +acc*	toward, against
adversus -a -um	contrary, unfavorable
aedificāre	build
aedificium -ī *n*	building
aeger -gra -grum	sick, ill
aegrōtāre	be ill
aegrōtus -a -um	sick
aequē	equally
aequinoctium -ī *n*	equinox
aequus -a -um	equal, calm
āēr -eris *m*	air
aestās -ātis *f*	summer
aestimāre	value, estimate
aetās -ātis *f*	age
affectus -ūs *m*	mood, feeling
af-ferre at-tulisse al-lātum	bring (to, forward, about)
af-ficere	affect, stir
af-firmāre	assert, affirm
age -ite *+imp*	come on! well, now
ager -grī *m*	field
agere ēgisse āctum	drive, do, perform
agmen -inis *n*	army on the march, file
agnus -ī *m*	lamb
agricola -ae *m*	farmer, peasant
ain'	you don't say? really?
āiō ais ait āiunt	say
āla -ae *f*	wing
albus -a -um	white
alere -uisse altum	feed
aliēnus -a -um	someone else's
ali-quandō	once
ali-quantum	a good deal
ali-quī -qua -quod	some
ali-quis -quid	someone, something
ali-quot *indēcl*	some, several
aliter	otherwise
alius -a -ud	another, other
aliī…aliī	some…others
allicere -iō -ēxisse -ectum	attract
alter -era -erum	one, the other, second
altum -ī *n*	the open sea
altus -a -um	high, tall, deep
amāns -antis *m*	lover
amāre	love
ambulāre	walk
amīca -ae *f*	girlfriend
amīcitia -ae *f*	friendship
amīcus -ī *m*	friend
amīcus -a -um	friendly
ā-mittere	lose
amnis -is *m*	river
amoenus -a -um	lovely, pleasant
amor -ōris *m*	love
amphitheātrum -ī *n*	amphitheater
an	or
ancilla -ae *f*	female slave, servant
angustus -a -um	narrow
anima -ae *f*	breath, life, soul
anim-ad-vertere	notice
animal -ālis *n*	animal, living being
animus -ī *m*	mind, soul
annus -ī *m*	year
ante *prp +acc, adv*	in front of, before
anteā	before, formerly
ante-hāc	formerly
ante-quam	before
antīquus -a -um	old, ancient, former
ānulus -ī *m*	ring
anus -ūs *f*	old woman
aperīre -uisse -rtum	open, disclose
apertus -a -um	open
apis -is *f*	bee

ap-pārēre	appear
appellāre	call, address
ap-pōnere	place (on), serve
ap-portāre	bring
ap-prehendere	seize
ap-propinquāre (+*dat*)	approach, come near
Aprīlis -is (mēnsis)	April
apud *prp +acc*	beside, near, by
aqua -ae *f*	water
aquila -ae *f*	eagle
arānea -ae *f*	spider, cobweb
arāre	plow
arātor -ōris *m*	plowman
arātrum -ī *n*	plough
arbitrārī	think, believe
arbor -oris *f*	tree
arcessere -īvisse -ītum	send for, fetch
arcus -ūs *m*	bow
arduus -a -um	steep
argenteus -a -um	silver-, of silver
argentum -ī *n*	silver
arma -ōrum *n pl*	arms
armāre	arm, equip
armātus -a -um	armed
ars artis *f*	art, skill
as assis *m*	as (copper coin)
a-scendere -disse	climb, go up, mount
asinīnus -a -um	ass's
asinus -ī *m*	ass, donkey
a-spergere -sisse -sum	sprinkle, scatter (on)
a-spicere	look at, look
at	but
āter -tra -trum	black, dark
atque/ac	and, as, than
ātrium -ī *n*	main room, hall
attentus -a -um	attentive
audācia -ae *f*	boldness, audacity
audāx -ācis *adi*	bold, audacious
audēre ausum esse	dare, venture
audīre	hear, listen
au-ferre abs-tulisse ablātum	carry off, take away
au-fugere	run away, escape
augēre -xisse -ctum	increase
Augustus -ī (mēnsis)	August
aureus -a -um	gold-, *m* gold piece
aurīga -ae *m*	charioteer, driver
auris -is *f*	ear
aurum -ī *n*	gold
aut	or
aut…aut	either…or
autem	but, however
autumnus -ī *m*	autumn
auxilium -ī *n*	help, assistance
auxilia -ōrum *n pl*	auxiliary forces
avārus -a -um	greedy, avaricious
ā-vertere	turn aside, avert
avis -is *f*	bird
avunculus -ī *m*	(maternal) uncle

B

baculum -ī *n*	stick
bālāre	bleat
balneum -ī *n*	bath, bathroom
barbarus -a -um	foreign, barbarian
bāsium -ī *n*	kiss
beātus -a -um	happy
bellum -ī *n*	war
bellus -a -um	lovely, pretty
bene	well
beneficium -ī *n*	benefit, favor
bēstia -ae *f*	beast, animal
bēstiola -ae *f*	small animal, insect
bibere -bisse	drink
bīnī -ae -a	two (each)
bis	twice
bonum -ī *n*	good, blessing
bonus -a -um	good
bōs bovis *m/f*	ox
bracchium -ī *n*	arm
brevī *adv*	soon
brevis -e	short

C

cachinnus -ī *m*	laugh, guffaw
cadere cecidisse	fall
caecus -a -um	blind
caedere cecīdisse caesum	beat, fell, kill
caedēs -is *f*	killing, slaughter
caelum -ī *n*	sky, heaven
calamus -ī *m*	reed, pen
calceus -ī *m*	shoe
calidus -a -um	warm, hot, *f* hot water
calor -ōris *m*	warmth, heat
campus -ī *m*	plain
candidus -a -um	white, bright
canere cecinisse	sing (of), crow, play
canis -is *m/f*	dog
cantāre	sing
cantus -ūs *m*	singing, music
capere -iō cēpisse captum	take, catch, capture
capillus -ī *m*	hair
capitulum -ī *n*	chapter
caput -itis *n*	head, chief, capital
carcer -eris *m*	prison
cardō -inis *m*	door pivot, hinge
carēre +*abl*	be without, lack
carmen -inis *n*	song, poem
carō carnis *f*	flesh, meat
carpere -psisse-ptum	gather, pick, crop
cārus -a -um	dear
castra -ōrum *n pl*	camp
cāsus -ūs *m*	fall, case

catēna -ae *f*	chain
cauda -ae *f*	tail
causa -ae *f*	cause, reason
gen (/meā) +causā	for the sake of
cautus -a -um	cautious
cavēre cāvisse cautum	beware (of)
cēdere cessisse	go, withdraw
celer -eris -ere	swift, quick
celsus -a -um	tall
cēna -ae *f*	dinner
cēnāre	dine, have dinner
cēnsēre -uisse -sum	think
centēsimus -a -um	hundredth
centum	a hundred
cēra -ae *f*	wax
cerebrum -ī *n*	brain
cernere crēvisse	discern, perceive
certāmen -inis *n*	contest, fight
certāre	contend, fight
certē	certainly, at any rate
certō *adv*	for certain
certus -a -um	certain, sure
cessāre	leave off, cease
cēterī -ae -a	the other(s), the rest
cēterum *adv*	besides, however
cēterus -a -um	remaining
charta -ae *f*	paper
cibus -ī *m*	food
cingere cīnxisse cīnctum	surround
-cipere -iō -cēpisse -ceptum	
circā *prp +acc*	round
circēnsēs -ium *m pl*	games in the circus
circēnsis -e	of the circus
circiter	about
circum *prp +acc*	round
circum-dare	surround
circum-silīre	hop about
circus -ī *m*	circle, orbit, circus
cis *prp +acc*	on this side of
citerior -ius *comp*	nearer
citrā *prp +acc*	on this side of
cīvis -is *m/f*	citizen, countryman
clāmāre	shout
clāmor -ōris *m*	shout, shouting
clārus -a -um	bright, clear, loud
classis -is *f*	fleet
claudere -sisse -sum	shut, close
claudus -a -um	lame
clausus -a -um	closed, shut
clāvis -is *f*	key
clēmēns -entis *adi*	mild, lenient
cocus -ī *m*	cook
coep- *v.* incipere	
cōgere co-ēgisse -āctum	compel, force
cōgitāre	think
cognōmen -inis *n*	surname
cognōscere -ōvisse -itum	get to know, recognize
cohors -rtis *f*	cohort
colere -uisse cultum	cultivate
collis -is *m*	hill
col-loquī	talk, converse
colloquium -ī *n*	conversation
collum -ī *n*	neck
colōnus -ī *m*	(tenant-) farmer
color -ōris *m*	color
columna -ae *f*	column
comes -itis *m*	companion
comitārī	accompany
com-memorāre	mention
commūnis -e	common
cōmoedia -ae *f*	comedy
com-parāre	compare
com-plectī -exum	embrace
com-plēre -ēvisse -ētum	fill, complete
com-plūrēs -a	several
com-putāre	calculate, reckon
cōnārī	attempt, try
condiciō -ōnis *f*	condition
cōn-ficere	make, accomplish
cōn-fidere *+dat*	trust
cōn-fitērī -fessum	confess
con-iungere	join, connect
coniūnx -iugis *m/f*	consort, wife
cōn-scendere -disse	mount, board
cōn-sequī	follow, overtake
cōn-sīdere -sēdisse	sit down
cōnsilium -ī *n*	advice, decision, intention, plan
cōn-sistere -stitisse	stop, halt
cōn-sōlārī	comfort, console
cōnsonāns -antis *f*	consonant
cōnspectus -ūs *m*	sight, view
cōn-spicere	catch sight of, see
cōnstāns -antis *adi*	steady, firm
cōn-stāre -stitisse	be fixed, cost
cōnstāre ex	consist of
cōn-stituere -uisse -ūtum	fix, decide
cōn-sūmere	spend, consume
con-temnere -mpsisse -mptum	despise, scorn
con-tinēre -uisse -tentum	contain
continuō *adv*	immediately
contrā *prp +acc*	against
con-trahere	draw together, wrinkle
contrārius -a -um	opposite, contrary
con-turbāre	mix up, confound
con-venīre	come together, meet
convenīre (ad/*+dat*)	fit, be fitting
con-vertere	turn
convīva -ae *m/f*	guest
convīvium -ī *n*	dinner-party
con-vocāre	call together

cōpia -ae *f*	abundance, lot	**dēlēre** -ēvisse -ētum	delete, efface
cōpulāre	join, connect	**dēliciae** -ārum *f pl*	delight, pet
coquere -xisse -ctum	cook	**delphīnus** -ī *m*	dolphin
cor cordis *n*	heart	**dēmere** -mpsisse -mptum	remove
cōram *prp +abl*	in the presence of	**dē-mōnstrāre**	point out, show
cornū -ūs *n*	horn	**dēmum** *adv*	at last, only
corpus -oris *n*	body	**dēnārius** -ī *m*	denarius (silver coin)
cor-rigere -rēxisse -rēctum	correct	**dēnī** -ae -a	ten (each)
cotīdiē	every day	**dēnique**	finally, at last
crās	tomorrow	**dēns** dentis *m*	tooth
crassus -a -um	thick, fat	**dē-nuō**	anew, again
crēdere -didisse *+dat*	believe, trust, entrust	**deorsum** *adv*	down
crēscere -ēvisse	grow	**dē-rīdēre**	laugh at, make fun of
cruciāre	torture, torment	**dē-scendere** -disse	go down, descend
crūdēlis -e	cruel	**dē-serere** -uisse -rtum	leave, desert
cruentus -a -um	blood-stained, bloody	**dēsīderāre**	long for, miss
cruor -ōris *m*	blood-stained, bloody	**dē-silīre** -uisse	jump down
crūs -ūris *n*	leg	**dē-sinere** -siisse	finish, stop, end
crux -ucis *f*	cross	**dē-sistere** -stitisse	leave off, cease
cubāre -uisse -itum	lie (in bed)	**dē-spērāre**	lose hope, despair (of)
cubiculum -ī *n*	bedroom	**dē-spicere**	look down (on), despise
culīna -ae *f*	kitchen	**dē-tergēre**	wipe off
culter -tri *m*	knife	**dē-terrēre**	deter
cum *prp +abl*	with	**dē-trahere**	pull off
cum *coniūnctiō*	when, as	**deus** -ī *m, pl* deī/diī/dī	god
cum prīmum *+perf*	as soon as	**dē-vorāre**	swallow up, devour
cūnae -ārum *f pl*	cradle	**dexter** -tra -trum	right, *f* the right (hand)
cūnctus -a -um	whole, *pl* all	**dīcere** -xisse dictum	say, call, speak
cupere -iō -īvisse	desire	**dictāre**	dictate
cupiditās -ātis *f*	desire	**dictum** -ī *n*	saying, words
cupidus -a -um (*+gen*)	desirous (of), eager (for)	**diēs** -ēī *m (f)*	day, date
cūr	why	**dif-ficilis** -e, *sup* -illimus	difficult, hard
cūra -ae *f*	care, anxiety	**digitus** -ī *m*	finger
cūrāre	care for, look after, take care	**dignus** -a -um	worthy
		dīligēns -entis *adi*	careful, diligent
currere cucurrisse	run	**dīligere** -ēxisse -ēctum	love, be fond of
currus -ūs *m*	chariot	**dīmidius** -a -um	half
cursus -ūs *m*	race, journey, course	**dī-mittere**	send away, dismiss
cūstōdīre	guard	**dīrus** -a -um	dreadful
		dis-cēdere	go away, depart
D		**discere** didicisse	learn
dare dedisse datum	give	**discipulus** -ī *m*	pupil, disciple
dē *prp +abl*	(down) from, of, about	**dis-iungere**	separate
dea -ae *f*	goddess	**dis-suādēre**	advise not to
dēbēre	owe, be obliged	**diū,** *comp* diūtius	long
dēbilis -e	weak	**dīves** -itis *adi*	rich, wealthy
decem	ten	**dīvidere** -īsisse -īsum	separate, divide
December -bris (mēnsis)	December	**dīvitiae** -ārum *f pl*	riches
decēre	be fitting, become	**docēre** -uisse doctum	teach, instruct
deciēs	ten times	**doctus** -a -um	learned, skilled
decimus -a -um	tenth	**dolēre**	hurt, feel pain, grieve
dēclīnāre	decline, inflect	**dolor** -ōris *m*	pain, grief
de-esse dē-fuisse (*+dat*)	be missing, fail	**domī** *loc*	at home
dē-fendere -disse -ēnsum	defend	**domina** -ae *f*	mistress
de-inde/dein	afterward, then	**dominus** -ī *m*	master
dēlectāre	delight, please	**domum** *adv*	home

domus -ūs *f, abl* -ō	house, home
dōnāre	give, present with
dōnec	as long as
dōnum -ī *n*	gift, present
dormīre	sleep
dorsum -ī *n*	back
dubitāre	doubt
dubius -a -um	undecided, doubtful
du-centī -ae -a	two hundred
dūcere -xisse ductum	guide, lead, draw, trace
uxōrem dūcere	marry
dulcis -e	sweet
dum	while, as long as, till
dum-modo	provided that, if only
dumtaxat	only, just
duo -ae -o	two
duo-decim	twelve
duo-decimus -a -um	twelfth
duo-dē-trīgintā	twenty-eight
duo-dē-vīgintī	eighteen
dūrus -a -um	hard
dux ducis *m*	leader, chief, general

E

ē *v.* ex/ē	
ēbrius -a -um	drunk
ecce	see, look, here is
ēducāre	bring up
ē-dūcere	bring out, draw out
ef-ficere	make, effect, cause
ef-fugere	escape, run away
ef-fundere	pour out, shed
ego mē mihi/mī	I, me, myself
ē-gredī -ior -gressum	go out
ēgregius -a -um	outstanding, excellent
ē-icere	throw out
ē-līdere -sisse -sum	omit, elide
ē-ligere -lēgisse -lēctum	choose, select
emere ēmisse ēmptum	buy
ēn	look, here is
enim	for
ēnsis -is *m*	sword
eō *adv*	to that place, there
epigramma -atis *n*	epigram
epistula -ae *f*	letter
eques -itis *m*	horseman
equidem	indeed, for my part
equitātus -ūs *m*	cavalry
equus -ī *m*	horse
ergā *prp +acc*	toward
ergō	therefore, so
ē-ripere -iō -uisse -reptum	snatch away, deprive of
errāre	wander, stray
ē-rubēscere -buisse	blush
ē-rumpere	break out
erus -ī *m*	master
esse sum fuisse futūrum esse/fore	be
ēsse edō ēdisse ēsum	eat
et	and, also
et…et	both…and
et-enim	and indeed, for
etiam	also, even, yet
etiam atque etiam	again and again
etiam-nunc	still
et-sī	even if, although
ē-volāre	fly out
ē-volvere -visse -lūtum	unroll
ex/ē *prp +abl*	out of, from, of, since
ex-audīre	hear
ex-citāre	wake up, arouse
ex-clāmāre	cry out, exclaim
ex-cōgitāre	think out, devise
ex-cruciāre	torture, torment
ex-currere -rrisse -rsum	run out, rush out
ex-cūsāre	excuse
exemplum -ī *n*	example, model
exercitus -ūs *m*	army
ex-haurīre	drain, empty
exiguus -a -um	small, scanty
ex-īre -eō -iisse -itum	go out
ex-īstimāre	consider, think
exitus -ūs *m*	exit, way out, end
ex-ōrnāre	adorn, decorate
ex-plānāre	explain
ex-pōnere	put out/ashore, expose
ex-pugnāre	conquer
ex-pugnātiō -ōnis *f*	conquest
ex-spectāre	wait (for), expect
ex-tendere -disse -tum	stretch out, extend
extrā *prp +acc*	outside

F

faber -brī *m*	artisan, smith
fābula -ae *f*	story, fable, play
fābulārī	talk, chat
facere -iō fēcisse factum	make, do, cause
faciēs -ēī *f*	face
facile *adv*	easily
facilis -e, *sup* -illimus	easy
factum -ī *n*	deed, act
fallāx -ācis *adi*	deceitful
fallere fefellisse falsum	deceive
falsus -a -um	false
falx -cis *f*	sickle
fāma -ae *f*	rumor, reputation
famēs -is *f*	hunger, famine
familia -ae *f*	domestic staff, family
fārī	speak
fatērī fassum	admit, confess
fatīgāre	tire out, weary
fātum -ī *n*	fate, destiny, death

favēre fāvisse +*dat* — favor, support
Februārius -ī (mēnsis) — February
fēlīcitās -ātis *f* — good fortune, luck
fēlīx -īcis *adi* — fortunate, lucky
fēmina -ae *f* — woman
fenestra -ae *f* — window
fera -ae *f* — wild animal
ferē — about, almost
ferōx -ōcis *adi* — fierce, ferocious
ferre tulisse lātum — carry, bring, bear
ferreus -a -um — of iron, iron-
ferrum -ī *n* — iron, steel
fertilis -e — fertile
ferus -a -um — wild
fessus -a -um — tired, weary
-ficere -iō -fēcisse -fectum
fīdere fīsum esse +*dat* — trust, rely on
fidēs -eī *f* — trust, faith, loyalty
fidēs -ium *f pl* — lyre
fidicen -inis *m* — lyre-player
fīdus -a -um — faithful, reliable
fierī factum esse — be made, be done, become, happen
fīgere -xisse -xum — fix, fasten
fīlia -ae *f* — daughter
fīliola -ae *f* — little daughter
fīliolus -ī *m* — little son
fīlius -ī *m* — son
fīlum -ī *n* — thread
fīnīre — limit, finish
fīnis -is *m* — boundary, limit, end
flāre — blow
flectere -xisse -xum — bend, turn
flēre -ēvisse — cry, weep (for)
flōs -ōris *m* — flower
flūctus -ūs *m* — wave
fluere -ūxisse — flow
flūmen -inis *n* — river
fluvius -ī *m* — river
foedus -a -um — ugly, hideous
folium -ī *n* — leaf
forās *adv* — out
foris -is *f* — leaf of a door, door
forīs *adv* — outside, out of doors
fōrma -ae *f* — form, shape, figure
fōrmōsus -a -um — beautiful
forsitan — perhaps, maybe
fortasse — perhaps, maybe
forte *adv* — by chance
fortis -e — strong, brave
fortūna -ae *f* — fortune
forum -ī *n* — square
fossa -ae *f* — ditch, trench
frangere frēgisse frāctum — break, shatter
frāter -tris *m* — brother
fremere -uisse — growl
frequēns -entis *adi* — numerous, frequent
fretum -ī *n* — strait
frīgēre — be cold
frīgidus -a -um — cold, chilly, cool
frīgus -oris *n* — cold
frōns -ontis *f* — forehead
frūgēs -um *f pl* — fruit, crops
fruī +*abl* — enjoy
frūmentum -ī *n* — corn, grain
frūstrā — in vain
fuga -ae *f* — flight
fugere -iō fūgisse — run away, flee
fugitīvus -a -um — runaway
fulgur -uris *n* — flash of lightning
fundere fūdisse fūsum — pour, shed
funditus *adv* — to the bottom, utterly
fundus -ī *m* — bottom
fūr -is *m* — thief
fūrtum -ī *n* — theft
futūrus -a -um (*v.* esse) — future
  tempus futūrum — future

G

gallus -ī *m* — cock, rooster
gaudēre gavīsum esse — be glad, be pleased
gaudium -ī *n* — joy, delight
geminus -a -um — twin
gemma -ae *f* — precious stone, jewel
gemmātus -a -um — set with a jewel
gena -ae *f* — cheek
gēns gentis *f* — nation, people
genū -ūs *n* — knee
genus -eris *n* — kind, sort
gerere gessisse gestum — carry, wear, carry on, do
glaciēs -ēī *f* — ice
gladiātor -ōris *m* — gladiator
gladiātōrius -a -um — gladiatorial
gladius -ī *m* — sword
glōria -ae *f* — glory
glōriōsus -a -um — glorious, boastful
gracilis -e — slender
gradus -ūs *m* — step, degree
Graecus -a -um — Greek
grammatica -ae *f* — grammar
grātia -ae *f* — favor, gratitude
  gen (/meā) + grātiā — for the sake of
  grātiam habēre — be grateful
  grātiās agere — thank
grātus -a -um — pleasing, grateful
gravida *adi f* — pregnant
gravis -e — heavy, severe, grave
gremium -ī *n* — lap
grex -egis *m* — flock, herd, band
gubernāre — steer, govern
gubernātor -ōris *m* — steersman
gustāre — taste

H	
habēre	have, hold, consider
habitāre	dwell, live
hasta -ae *f*	lance
haud	not
haurīre -sisse -stum	draw (water), bail
herba -ae *f*	grass, herb
herī	yesterday
heu	o! alas!
heus	hey! hello!
hic haec hoc	this
hīc	here
hiems -mis *f*	winter
hinc	from here, hence
hodiē	today
holus -eris *n*	vegetable
homō -inis *m*	human being, person
hōra -ae *f*	hour
horrendus -a -um	dreadful
horrēre	bristle, stand on end, shudder (at)
hortārī	encourage, urge
hortus -ī *m*	garden
hospes -itis *m*	guest, guest-friend
hostis -is *m*	enemy
hūc	here, to this place
hūmānus -a -um	human
humī *loc*	on the ground
humilis -e	low
humus -ī *f*	ground
I	
iacere -iō iēcisse iactum	throw, hurl
iacēre	lie
iactāre	throw, toss about
iactūra -ae *f*	throwing away, loss
iam	now, already
iānitor -ōris *m*	doorkeeper
iānua -ae *f*	door
Iānuārius -ī (mēnsis)	January
ibi	there
-icere -iō -iēcisse -iectum	
īdem eadem idem	the same
id-eō	for that reason
idōneus -a -um	fit, suitable
īdūs -uum *f pl*	13th/15th (of the month)
iecur -oris *n*	liver
igitur	therefore, then, so
ignārus -a -um	ignorant, unaware
ignis -is *m*	fire
ignōrāre	not know
ignōscere -ōvisse +*dat*	forgive
ignōtus -a -um	unknown
ille -a -ud	that, the one, he
illīc	there
illinc	from there
illūc	there, thither
illūstrāre	illuminate, make clear
imāgō -inis *f*	picture
imber -bris *m*	rain, shower
imitārī	imitate
im-mātūrus -a -um	unripe
immō	no, on the contrary
im-mortālis -e	immortal
im-pār -aris *adi*	unequal
im-patiēns -entis *adi*	impatient
im-pendēre +*dat*	threaten
imperāre +*dat*	command, order, rule
imperātor -ōris *m*	(commanding) general
imperium -ī *n*	command, empire
impetus -ūs *m*	attack, charge
im-piger -gra -grum	active, industrious
im-plēre -ēvisse -ētum	fill, complete
im-plicāre -uisse -itum	enfold
impluvium -ī *n*	water basin
im-pōnere	place (in/on), put
im-primere -pressisse -pressum	press (into)
im-probus -a -um	bad, wicked
īmus -a -um *sup*	lowest
in *prp +abl*	in, on, at
prp +acc	into, to, against
in-certus -a -um	uncertain
in-cipere -iō coepisse coeptum	begin
in-clūdere -sisse -sum	shut up
incola -ae *m/f*	inhabitant
in-colere	inhabit
incolumis -e	unharmed, safe
inconditus -a -um	unpolished, rough
inde	from there, thence
index -icis *m*	list, catalogue
in-dignus -a -um	unworthy, shameful
in-doctus -a -um	ignorant
induere -uisse -ūtum	put on (clothes)
indūtus +*abl*	dressed in
industrius -a -um	industrious
in-ermis -e	unarmed
in-esse	be (in)
in-exspectātus -a -um	unexpected
īnfāns -antis *m/f*	little child, baby
īn-fēlīx -īcis *adi*	unlucky, unfortunate
īnferior -ius *comp*	lower, inferior
īnferus -a -um	lower
Īnferī -ōrum *m pl*	the underworld
īnfēstus -a -um	unsafe, infested
īn-fidus -a -um	faithless
īnfimus -a -um *sup*	lowest
īn-fluere	flow into
īnfrā *prp +acc*	below
ingenium -ī *n*	nature, character

ingēns -entis *adi*	huge, vast
in-hūmānus -a -um	inhuman
in-imīcus -ī *m*	(personal) enemy
in-inimīcus -a -um	unfriendly
initium -ī *n*	beginning
iniūria -ae *f*	injustice, wrong
in-iūstus -a -um	unjust, unfair
inopia -ae *f*	lack, scarcity
inquit -iunt	(he/she) says/said
inquam	I say
īn-scrībere	write on, inscribe
īnscrīptiō -ōnis *f*	inscription
īn-struere -ūxisse -ūctum	draw up, arrange
īnstrūmentum -ī *n*	tool, instrument
īnsula -ae *f*	island
integer -gra -grum	undamaged, intact
intellegere -ēxisse -ēctum	understand, realize
inter *prp +acc*	between, among, during
inter sē	(with) one another
inter-dum	now and then
inter-eā	meanwhile
inter-esse	be between
inter-ficere	kill
interim	meanwhile
internus -a -um	inner, internal
inter-pellāre	interrupt
inter-rogāre	ask, question
intrā *prp +acc*	inside, within
intrāre	enter
intuērī	look at, watch
intus *adv*	inside
in-validus -a -um	infirm, weak
in-vehere	import
in-venīre	find
in-vidēre *+dat*	envy, grudge
invidia -ae *f*	envy
in-vocāre	call upon, invoke
iocōsus -a -um	humorous, funny
ipse -a -um	himself
īra -ae *f*	anger
īrātus -a -um	angry
īre eō iisse itum	go
is ea id	he, she, it, that
iste -a -ud	this, that (of yours)
ita	so, in such a way
ita-que	therefore
item	likewise, also
iter itineris *n*	journey, march, way
iterum	again, a second time
iubēre iussisse iussum	order, tell
iūcundus -a -um	pleasant, delightful
Iūlius -ī (mēnsis)	July
iungere iūnxisse iūnctum	join, combine
Iūnius -ī (mēnsis)	June
iūs iūris *n*	right, justice
iūre	justly, rightly
iūstus -a -um	just, fair
iuvāre iūvisse iūtum	help, delight
iuvenis -is *m*	young man
iūxtā *prp +acc*	next to, beside

K

kalendae -ārum *f pl*	the 1st (of the month)
kalendārium -ī *n*	calendar

L

lābī lāpsum	slip, drop, fall
labor -ōris *m*	work, toil
labōrāre	toil, work, take trouble
labrum -ī *n*	lip
labyrinthus -ī *m*	labyrinth
lac lactis *n*	milk
lacertus -ī *m*	(upper) arm
lacrima -ae *f*	tear
lacrimāre	shed tears, weep
lacus -ūs *m*	lake
laedere -sisse -sum	injure, hurt
laetārī	rejoice, be glad
laetitia -ae *f*	joy
laetus -a -um	glad, happy
laevus -a -um	left
lāna -ae *f*	wool
largīrī	give generously
largus -a -um	generous
latēre	be hidden, hide
Latīnus -a -um	Latin
lātrāre	bark
latus -eris *n*	side, flank
lātus -a -um	broad, wide
laudāre	praise
laus laudis *f*	praise
lavāre lāvisse lautum	wash, bathe
lectīca -ae *f*	litter, sedan
lectulus -ī *m*	(little) bed
lectus -ī *m*	bed, couch
lēgātus -ī *m*	envoy, delegate
legere lēgisse lēctum	read
legiō -ōnis *f*	legion
legiōnārius -a -um	legionary
leō -ōnis *m*	lion
levāre	lift, raise
levis -e	light, slight
lēx lēgis *f*	law
libellus -ī *m*	little book
libenter	with pleasure, gladly
liber -brī *m*	book
līber -era -erum	free
līberāre	free, set free
libēre: libet *+dat*	it pleases
līberī -ōrum *m pl*	children
lībertās -ātis *f*	freedom, liberty
lībertīnus -ī *m*	freedman

licēre: licet *+dat*	it is allowed, one may
ligneus -a -um	wooden
lignum -ī *n*	wood
līlium -ī *n*	lily
līmen -inis *n*	threshold
līnea -ae *f*	string, line
lingua -ae *f*	tongue, language
littera -ae *f*	letter
lītus -oris *n*	beach, shore
locus -ī *m*	place
loca -ōrum *n pl*	regions, parts
longē	far, by far
longus -a -um	long
loquī locūtum	speak, talk
lūcēre lūxisse	shine
lucerna -ae *f*	lamp
lucrum -ī *n*	profit, gain
luctārī	wrestle
lūdere -sisse -sum	play
lūdus -ī *m*	play, game, school
lūgēre -xisse	mourn
lūna -ae *f*	moon
lupus -ī *m*	wolf
lūx lūcis *f*	light, daylight

M

maerēre	grieve
maestus -a -um	sad, sorrowful
magis	more
magister -tri *m*	schoolmaster, teacher
magnificus -a -um	magnificent, splendid
magnus -a -um	big, large, great
māior -ius *comp*	bigger, older
Māius -ī (mēnsis)	May
male *adv*	badly, ill
maleficium -ī *n*	evil deed, crime
mālle māluisse	prefer
malum -ī *n*	evil, trouble, harm
mālum -ī *n*	apple
malus -a -um	bad, wicked, evil
mamma -ae *f*	mummy
māne *indēcl n, adv*	morning, in the morning
manēre mānsisse	remain, stay
manus -ūs *f*	hand
mare -is *n*	sea
margarīta -ae *f*	pearl
maritimus -a -um	sea-, coastal
marītus -ī *m*	husband
Mārtius -ī (mēnsis)	March
māter -tris *f*	mother
māteria -ae *f*	material, substance
mātrōna -ae *f*	married woman
mātūrus -a -um	ripe
māximē	most, especially
māximus -a -um	biggest, greatest, oldest
medicus -ī *m*	physician, doctor
medium -ī *n*	middle, center
medius -a -um	mid, middle
mel mellis *n*	honey
melior -ius *comp*	better
mellītus -a -um	sweet
membrum -ī *n*	limb
meminisse *+gen/acc*	remember, recollect
memorāre	mention
memoria -ae *f*	memory
mendum -ī *n*	mistake, error
mēns mentis *f*	mind
mēnsa -ae *f*	table
mēnsa secunda	dessert
mēnsis -is *m*	month
mentiō -ōnis *f*	mention
mentīrī	lie
mercātor -ōris *m*	merchant
mercātōrius -a -um	merchant-
mercēs -ēdis *f*	wage, fee, rent
merēre	earn, deserve
mergere -sisse -sum	dip, plunge, sink
merīdiēs -ēī *m*	midday, noon, south
merum -ī *n*	neat wine
merus -a -um	pure, neat, undiluted
merx -rcis *f*	commodity, *pl* goods
metere	reap, harvest
metuere -uisse	fear
metus -ūs *m*	fear
meus -a -um, *voc* mī	my, mine
mīles -itis *m*	soldier
mīlitāre	serve as a soldier
mīlitāris -e	military
mīlle, *pl* mīlia -ium *n*	thousand
minārī *+dat*	threaten
minimē	by no means, not at all
minimus -a -um *sup*	smallest, youngest
minister -trī *m*	servant
minor -us *comp*	smaller, younger
minuere -uisse -ūtum	diminish, reduce
minus -ōris *n, adv*	less
mīrābilis -e	marvelous, wonderful
mīrārī	wonder (at), be surprised
mīrus -a -um	surprising, strange
miscēre -uisse mixtum	mix
misellus -a -um	poor, wretched
miser -era -erum	unhappy, miserable
mittere mīsisse missum	send, throw
modo	only, just
modo…modo	now…now
modus -ī *m*	manner, way
nūllō modō	by no means
moenia -ium *n pl*	walls
molestus -a -um	troublesome
mollīre	make soft, soften

mollis -e	soft
monēre	remind, advise, warn
mōns montis *m*	mountain
mōnstrāre	point out, show
mōnstrum -ī *n*	monster
mora -ae *f*	delay
mordēre momordisse -sum	bite
morī mortuum	die
mors mortis *f*	death
mortālis -e	mortal
mortuus -a -um (< morī)	dead
mōs mōris *m*	custom, usage
movēre mōvisse mōtum	move, stir
mox	soon
mulier -eris *f*	woman
multī -ae -a	many, a great many
multitūdō -inis *f*	large number, multitude
multō *+comp*	much, by far
multum -ī *n, adv*	much
mundus -ī *m*	world, universe
mundus -a -um	clean, neat
mūnīre	fortify
mūnus -eris *n*	gift
mūrus -ī *m*	wall
Mūsa -ae *f*	Muse
mūtāre	change, exchange
mūtus -a -um	dumb
mūtuus -a -um	on loan
mūtuum dare/sūmere	lend/borrow

N

nam	**for**
-nam	…ever?
namque	for
nārrāre	relate, tell
nārrātiō -ōnis *f*	narrative
nāscī nātum	be born
nāsus -ī *m*	nose
natāre	swim
nātūra -ae *f*	nature
nātus -a -um (< nāscī)	born
XX annōs nātus	20 years old
nauta -ae *m*	sailor
nāvicula -ae *f*	boat
nāvigāre	sail
nāvigātiō -ōnis *f*	sailing, voyage
nāvis -is *f*	ship
-ne	…? if, whether
nē	that not, lest, that
nē…quidem	not even
nec *v.* ne-que/nec	
necāre	kill
necessārius -a -um	necessary
necesse est	it is necessary
negāre	deny, say that…not
neglegēns -entis *adi*	careless
neglegere -ēxisse -ēctum	neglect
negōtium -ī *n*	business, activity
nēmō -inem -inī	no one, nobody
nēquam *adi indēcl, sup* nēquissimus	worthless, bad
ne-que/nec	and/but not, nor, not
n….n.	neither…nor
ne-scīre	not know
neu *v.* nē-ve/neu	
neuter -tra -trum	neither
nē-ve/neu	and (that) not, nor
nex necis *f*	killing, murder
nīdus -ī *m*	nest
niger -gra -grum	black
nihil/nīl	nothing
nimis	too, too much
nimium	too much
nimius -a -um	too big
nisi	if not, except, but
niveus -a -um	snow-white
nix nivis *f*	snow
nōbilis -e	well known, famous
nocēre *+dat*	harm, hurt
nōlī -īte *+īnf*	don't…!
nōlle nōluisse	be unwilling, not want
nōmen -inis *n*	name
nōmināre	name, call
nōn	not
nōnae -ārum *f pl*	5th/7th (of the month)
nōnāgēsimus -a -um	ninetieth
nōnāgintā	ninety
nōn-dum	not yet
nōn-gentī -ae -a	nine hundred
nōn-ne	not?
nōn-nūllī -ae -a	some, several
nōn-numquam	sometimes
nōnus -a -um	ninth
nōs nōbīs	we, us, ourselves
nōscere nōvisse	get to know, *perf* know
noster -tra -trum	our, ours
nostrum *gen*	of us
nota -ae *f*	mark, sign
nōtus -a -um	known
novem	nine
November -bris (mēnsis)	November
nōvisse (< nōscere)	know
novus -a -um	new
nox noctis *f*	night
nūbere -psisse *+dat*	marry
nūbēs -is *f*	cloud
nūbilus -a -um	cloudy
nūdus -a -um	naked
nūgae -ārum *f pl*	idle talk, rubbish
nūllus -a -um	no
num	…? if, whether
numerāre	count

numerus -ī *m*	number
nummus -ī *m*	coin, sesterce
numquam	never
nunc	now
nūntiāre	announce, report
nūntius -ī *m*	messenger, message
nūper	recently
nūtrīx -īcis *f*	nurse
nux nucis *f*	nut

O

ō	**o!**
ob *prp +acc*	on account of
oblīvīscī -lītum *+gen/acc*	forget
ob-oedīre *+dat*	obey
obscūrus -a -um	dark
occidēns -entis *m*	west
oc-cidere -disse	fall, sink, set
oc-cīdere - disse -sum	kill
occultāre	hide
oc-currere -rrisse *+dat*	meet
ōceanus -ī *m*	ocean
ocellus -ī *m*	(little) eye
octāvus -a -um	eighth
octin-gentī -ae -a	eight hundred
octō	eight
Octōber -bris (mēnsis)	October
octōgintā	eighty
oculus -ī *m*	eye
ōdisse	hate
odium -ī *n*	hatred
of-ferre ob-tulisse oblātum	offer
officium -ī *n*	duty, task
ōlim	once, long ago
omnis -e	all, every
opera -ae *f*	effort, pains
operīre -uisse -ertum	cover
opēs -um *f pl*	resources, wealth
oportēre: oportet	it is right, you should
opperīrī -ertum	wait (for), await
oppidum -ī *n*	town
op-pugnāre	attack
optāre	wish
optimus -a -um *sup*	best, very good
opus -eris *n*	work
opus est	it is needed
ōra -ae *f*	border, coast
ōrāre	pray, beg
ōrātiō -ōnis *f*	speech
orbis -is *m*	circle, orbit
orbis terrārum	the world
ōrdināre	arrange, regulate
ōrdō -inis *m*	row, rank, order
oriēns -entis *m*	east
orīrī ortum	rise, appear
ōrnāmentum -ī *n*	ornament, jewel
ōrnāre	equip, adorn
os ossis *n*	bone
ōs ōris *n*	mouth
ōscitāre	gape, yawn
ōsculārī	kiss
ōsculum -ī *n*	kiss
ostendere -disse	show
ōstiārius -ī *m*	door-keeper, porter
ōstium -ī *n*	door, entrance
ōtiōsus -a -um	leisured, idle
ōtium -ī *n*	leisure
ovis -is *f*	sheep
ōvum -ī *n*	egg

P

pābulum -ī *n*	fodder
paene	nearly, almost
paen-īnsula -ae *f*	peninsula
pāgina -ae *f*	page
pallēre	be pale
pallidus -a -um	pale
pallium -ī *n*	cloak, mantle
palma -ae *f*	palm
palpitāre	beat, throb
pānis -is *m*	bread, loaf
pap*rus -ī *f*	papyrus
pār paris *adi*	equal
parāre	prepare, make ready
parātus -a -um	ready
parcere pepercisse *+dat*	spare
parentēs -um *m pl*	parents
parere -iō peperisse	give birth to, lay
pārēre (*+dat*)	obey
parricīda -ae *m*	parricide
pars -rtis *f*	part, direction
partīrī	share, divide
parum	too little, not quite
parvulus -a -um	little, tiny
parvus -a -um	little, small
pāscere pāvisse pāstum	pasture, feed, feast
passer -eris *m*	sparrow
passus -ūs *m*	pace (1.48 m)
pāstor -ōris *m*	shepherd
pater -tris *m*	father
patēre	be open
patī passum	suffer, undergo, bear
patiēns -entis *adi*	patient
patientia -ae *f*	forbearance, patience
patria -ae *f*	native country/town
paucī -ae -a	few, a few
paulisper	for a short time
paulō *+comp, ante/post*	a little
paulum	a little, little
pauper -eris *adi*	poor
pāx pācis *f*	peace
pectus -oris *n*	breast

pecūlium -ī *n*	money given to slaves
pecūnia -ae *f*	money
pecūniōsus -a -um	wealthy
pecus -oris *n*	livestock, sheep, cattle
pedes -itis *m*	foot-soldier
pēior -ius *comp*	worse
pellere pepulisse pulsum	push, drive (off)
penna -ae *f*	feather
pēnsum -ī *n*	task
per *prp +acc*	through, by, during
per-currere -rrisse -rsum	run over, pass over
per-cutere -iō -cussisse -cussum	strike, hit
per-dere -didisse -ditum	destroy, ruin, waste
per-ferre	carry, endure
per-ficere	complete, accomplish
pergere per-rēxisse	proceed, go on
perīculōsus -a -um	dangerous, perilous
perīculum -ī *n*	danger, peril
per-īre -eō -iisse	perish, be lost
perist*lum -ī *n*	peristyle
per-mittere	allow, permit
per-movēre	move deeply
perpetuus -a -um	continuous, permanent
per-sequī	follow, pursue
persōna -ae *f*	character, person
per-suādēre -sisse *+dat*	persuade, convince
per-territus -a -um	terrified
per-turbāre	upset
per-venīre	get to, reach
pēs pedis *m*	foot
pessimus -a -um *sup*	worst
petasus -ī *m*	hat
petere -īvisse -ītum	make for, aim at, attack, seek, ask for, request
phantasma -atis *n*	ghost, apparition
piger -gra -grum	lazy
pila -ae *f*	ball
pīlum -ī *n*	spear, javelin
pīpiāre	chirp
pīrāta -ae *m*	pirate
pirum -ī *n*	pear
piscātor -ōris *m*	fisherman
piscis -is *m*	fish
placēre *+dat*	please
plānē	plainly, clearly
plānus -a -um	plain, clear
plaudere -sisse (*+dat*)	clap, applaud
plēnus -a -um (*+gen/abl*)	full (of)
plērī-que plērae- plēra-	most, most people
plērumque	mostly
plōrāre	cry
plūrēs -a *comp*	more
plūrimī -ae -a *sup*	most, a great many
plūs plūris *n, adv*	more
pōculum -ī *n*	cup, glass

poena -ae *f*	punishment, penalty
poēta -ae *m/f*	poet
poēticus -a -um	poetical
pollicērī	promise
pōnere posuisse positum	place, put, lay down
populus -ī *m*	people, nation
porcus -ī *m*	pig
porta -ae *f*	gate
portāre	carry
portus -ūs *m*	harbor
poscere poposcisse	demand, call for
posse potuisse	be able
possidēre -sēdisse	possess, own
post *prp +acc, adv*	behind, after, later
post-eā	afterward, later
posterior -ius *comp*	back-, hind-, later
posterus -a -um	next, following
posthāc	from now on, hereafter
post-quam	after, since
postrēmō *adv*	finally
postrēmus -a -um *sup*	last
postulāre	demand, require
pōtāre	drink
potestās -ātis *f*	power
pōtiō -ōnis *f*	drinking, drink
potius	rather
prae *prp +abl*	before, for
praecipuē	especially, above all
praedium -ī *n*	estate
praedō -ōnis *m*	robber, pirate
prae-esse (*+dat*)	be in charge (of)
prae-ferre	prefer
praemium -ī *n*	reward, prize
prae-nōmen -inis *n*	first name
prae-pōnere *+dat*	put before/in charge of
praesēns -entis *adi*	present
prae-stāre -stitisse	furnish, fulfill
praeter *prp +acc*	past, besides, except
praeter-eā	besides
praeteritus -a -um	past
prāvus -a -um	faulty, wrong
precārī	pray
precēs -um *f pl*	prayers
prehendere -disse -ēnsum	grasp, seize
premere pressisse pressum	press
pretiōsus -a -um	precious
pretium -ī *n*	price, value
prīdem	long ago
prī-diē	the day before
prīmō *adv*	at first
prīmum *adv*	first
prīmus -a -um	first
prīnceps -ipis *m*	chief, leader
prīncipium -ī *n*	beginning
prior -ius	first, former, front-
prius *adv*	before

prius-quam	before
prīvātus -a -um	private
prō *prp +abl*	for, instead of
probus -a -um	good, honest, proper
prō-cēdere	go forward, advance
procul	far (from), far away
prō-currere -rrisse -rsum	run forward, charge
prōd-esse prō-fuisse *+dat*	be useful, do good
proelium -ī *n*	battle
profectō	indeed, certainly
prō-ferre	bring forth, produce
proficīscī -fectum	set out, depart
prō-gredī -ior -gressum	go forward, advance
pro-hibēre	keep off, prevent
prō-icere	throw (forward)
prōmere -mpsisse -mptum	take out
prōmissum -ī *n*	promise
prō-mittere	promise
prope *prp +acc, adv*	near, nearly
properāre	hurry
propinquus -a -um	near, close
proprius -a -um	own, proper
propter *prp +acc*	because of
propter-eā	therefore
prō-silīre -uisse	spring forth
prō-spicere	look out, look ahead
prōtinus	at once
prōvincia -ae *f*	province
proximus -a -um *sup*	nearest
prūdēns -entis *adi*	prudent, clever
pūblicus -a -um	public, State-
pudēre: pudet mē (*+gen*)	I am ashamed (of)
pudor -ōris *m*	(sense of) shame
puella -ae *f*	girl
puer -erī *m*	boy
pugna -ae *f*	fight
pugnāre	fight
pugnus -ī *m*	fist
pulcher -chra -chrum	beautiful, fine
pulchritūdō -inis *f*	beauty
pullus -ī *m*	young (of an animal)
pulmō -ōnis *m*	lung
pulsāre	strike, hit, knock (at)
pūnīre	punish
puppis -is *f*	stern, poop
pūrus -a -um	clean, pure
putāre	think, suppose

Q

quadrāgēsimus -a -um	fortieth
quadrāgintā	forty
quadrin-gentī -ae -a	four hundred
quaerere -sīvisse -sītum	look for, seek, ask (for)
quālis -e	what sort of, (such) as
quālitās -ātis *f*	quality
quam	how, as, than
quam *+sup*	as…as possible
quam-diū	how long, (as long) as
quam-ob-rem	why
quamquam	although
quandō	when, as
quantitās -ātis *f*	quantity, size
quantum -ī *n*	how much, (as much) as
quantus -a -um	how large, (as large) as
quā-propter	why
quā-rē	why
quārtus -a -um	fourth
quārta pars	fourth, quarter
quasi	as, like, as if
quater	four times
quatere -iō	shake
quaternī -ae -a	four (each)
quattuor	four
quattuor-decim	fourteen
-que	and
querī questum	complain, grumble
quī quae quod	who, which, he who
quī quae quod (…?)	what, which
quia	because
quid *n* (*v.* quis)	what, anything
quid *adv*	why
quī-dam quae- quod-	a certain, some
quidem	indeed, certainly
nē quidem	not even
quidnī	why not
quid-quam	anything
neque/nec quidquam	and nothing
quid-quid	whatever, anything that
quiēscere -ēvisse	rest
quiētus -a -um	quiet
quīn	why not, do…!
quīn-decim	fifteen
quīn-gentī -ae -a	five hundred
quīnī -ae -a	five (each)
quīnquāgintā	fifty
quīnque	five
quīnquiēs	five times
Quīntīlis -is (mēnsis)	July
quīntus -a -um	fifth
quis quae quid	who, what
quis quid (sī/num/nē…)	anyone, anything
quis-nam quid-nam	who/what ever?
quis-quam	anyone
neque/nec quisquam	and no one
quis-que quae- quod-	each
quis-quis	whoever, anyone who
quō *adv*	where (to)
quod (= quia)	because, that
quod *n* (*v.* quī)	what, which, that which
quō-modo	how

quoniam	as, since
quoque	also, too
quot *indēcl*	how many, (as many) as
quot-annīs	every year
quotiēs	how many times

R

rāmus -ī *m*	branch, bough
rapere -iō -uisse -ptum	tear away, carry off
rapidus -a -um	rushing, rapid
rārō *adv*	rarely, seldom
rārus -a -um	rare
ratiō -ōnis *f*	reason
ratis -is *f*	raft
re-cēdere	go back, retire
re-cipere	receive, admit
recitāre	read aloud
re-cognōscere	recognize
rēctus -a -um	straight, correct
rēctā (viā)	straight
re-cumbere -cubuisse	lie down
red-dere -didisse -ditum	give back, give
red-imere -ēmisse -ēmptum	ransom
red-īre -eō -iisse -itum	go back, return
re-dūcere	lead back, bring back
re-ferre rettulisse	bring back, return
regere rēxisse rēctum	direct, guide, govern
regiō -ōnis *f*	region, district
rēgnāre	reign, rule
rēgula -ae *f*	ruler
re-linquere -līquisse -lictum	leave
reliquus -a -um	remaining, left
re-manēre	remain, stay behind
rēmigāre	row
re-minīscī *+gen/acc*	recollect
re-mittere	send back
re-movēre	remove
rēmus -ī *m*	oar
repente	suddenly
reperīre repperisse repertum	find
re-pōnere	put back
re-prehendere	blame, censure
re-pugnāre	fight back, resist
re-quiēscere	rest
re-quīrere -sīvisse -sītum	seek, ask
rēs reī *f*	thing, matter, affair
re-sistere -stitisse *+dat*	halt, resist
re-spondēre -disse -sum	answer
respōnsum -ī *n*	answer
rēte -is *n*	net
re-tinēre -uisse -tentum	hold back
re-trahere	pull back, bring back
re-venīre	come back
revertī -tisse -sum	return, come back
re-vocāre	call back, revoke
rēx rēgis *m*	king
rīdēre -sisse -sum	laugh, make fun of
rīdiculus -a -um	ridiculous
rigāre	irrigate
rīpa -ae *f*	bank
rīsus -ūs *m*	laughter, laugh
rīvus -ī *m*	brook
rogāre	ask, ask for
rogitāre	ask (repeatedly)
Rōmānus -a -um	Roman
rosa -ae *f*	rose
ruber -bra -brum	red
rubēre	be red, blush
rudis -e	crude, rude
rūmor -ōris *m*	rumor
rumpere rūpisse ruptum	break
rūrī *loc*	in the country
rūrsus	again
rūs rūris *n*	the country
rūsticus -a -um	rural, rustic, farm-

S

sacculus -ī *m*	purse
saccus -ī *m*	sack
sacerdōs -ōtis *m/f*	priest, priestess
saeculum -ī *n*	century
saepe	often
saevus -a -um	fierce, cruel
sagitta -ae *f*	arrow
sāl salis *m*	salt, wit
salīre -uisse	jump
salūs -ūtis *f*	safety, well-being
salūtem dīcere *+dat*	greet
salūtāre	greet
salvāre	save
salvē -ēte	hallo, good morning
salvēre iubēre	greet
salvus -a -um	safe, unharmed
sānāre	heal, cure
sānē	certainly, quite
sanguis -inis *m*	blood
sānus -a -um	healthy, well
sapere -iō -iisse	be wise, have sense
sapiēns -entis *adi*	wise
satis	enough, rather
saxum -ī *n*	rock
scaena -ae *f*	scene, stage
scaenicus -a -um	theatrical
scalpellum -ī *n*	scalpel, surgical knife
scamnum -ī *n*	stool
scelestus -a -um	criminal, wicked
scelus -eris *n*	crime
scīlicet	of course
scindere scidisse scissum	tear, tear up

scīre	know
scrībere -psisse -ptum	write
scūtum -ī *n*	shield
sē sibi	himself
secāre -uisse -ctum	cut
secundum *prp +acc*	along
secundus -a -um	second, favorable
sed	but
sē-decim	sixteen
sedēre sēdisse	sit
sella -ae *f*	stool, chair
semel	once
sēmen -inis *n*	seed
semper	always
senex senis *m*	old man
sēnī -ae -a	six (each)
sententia -ae *f*	opinion, sentence
sentīre sēnsisse sēnsum	feel, sense, think
septem	seven
September -bris (mēnsis)	September
septen-decim	seventeen
septentriōnēs -um *m pl*	north
septimus -a -um	seventh
septin-gentī -ae -a	seven hundred
septuāgintā	seventy
sequī secūtum	follow
serēnus -a -um	clear, cloudless
serere sēvisse satum	sow, plant
sērius -a -um	serious
sermō -ōnis *m*	talk, conversation
servāre	preserve, save
servīre *+dat*	be a slave, serve
servitūs -ūtis *f*	slavery
servus -ī *m*	slave, servant
ses-centī -ae -a	six hundred
sēsē	himself
sēstertius -ī *m*	sesterce (coin)
seu *v.* sī-ve/seu	
sevērus -a -um	stern, severe
sex	six
sexāgintā	sixty
sexiēs	six times
Sextīlis -is (mēnsis)	August
sextus -a -um	sixth
sī	if
sīc	in this way, so, thus
siccus -a -um	dry
sīc-ut	just as, as
signāre	mark, seal
significāre	indicate, mean
significātiō -ōnis *f*	meaning, sense
signum -ī *n*	sign, seal, statue
silentium -ī *n*	silence
silēre	be silent
silva -ae *f*	wood, forest
similis -e	similar, like
simul	together, at the same time
simul atque *+perf*	as soon as
sīn	but if
sine *prp +abl*	without
sinere sīvisse situm	let, allow
singulī -ae -a	one (each), each
sinister -tra -trum	left, *f* the left (hand)
sinus -ūs *m*	fold (of toga)
sī-quidem	seeing that, since
sitis -is *f*	thirst
situs -a -um	situated
sī-ve/seu	or, or if
s. … s.	whether…or
sōl -is *m*	sun
solēre -itum esse	be accustomed
solum -ī *n*	soil, ground, floor
sōlum *adv*	only
sōlus -a -um	alone, lonely
solvere -visse solūtum	untie, discharge, pay
nāvem solvere	cast off, set sail
somnus -ī *m*	sleep
sonus -ī *m*	sound, noise
sordēs -ium *f pl*	dirt
sordidus -a -um	dirty, mean, base
soror -ōris *f*	sister
spargere -sisse -sum	scatter
speciēs -ēī *f*	appearance, aspect, sort
spectāre	watch, look at
spectātor -ōris *m*	spectator
speculum -ī *n*	mirror
spērāre	hope (for)
spēs -eī *f*	hope
-spicere -iō -spexisse -spectum	
spīrāre	breathe
stāre stetisse	stand
statim	at once
statuere -uisse -ūtum	fix, determine
stēlla -ae *f*	star
sternere strāvisse strātum	spread
stilus -ī *m*	stylus
stipendium -ī *n*	soldier's pay, service
strepitus -ūs *m*	noise, din
studēre *+dat*	devote oneself to
studiōsus -a -um (*+gen*)	interested (in)
studium -ī *n*	interest, study
stultus -a -um	stupid, foolish
stupēre	be aghast
suādēre -sisse *+dat*	advise
sub *prp +abl/acc*	under, near
sub-īre -eō -iisse	go under, undergo
subitō *adv*	suddenly
subitus -a -um	sudden
sub-mergere	sink
sub-urbānus -a -um	near the city
sūmere -mpsisse -mptum	take

summus -a -um *sup*	highest, greatest
super *prp +acc*	on (top of), above
prp +abl	on, about
superbus -a -um	haughty, proud
super-esse	be left, be in excess
superior -ius *comp*	higher, upper, superior
superus -a -um	upper
supplicium -ī *n*	(capital) punishment
suprā *prp +acc, adv*	above
surdus -a -um	deaf
surgere sur-rēxisse	rise, get up
sur-ripere -iō -uisse -reptum	steal
sūrsum	up, upward
suscitāre	wake up, rouse
su-spicere	look up (at)
sus-tinēre	support, sustain, endure
suus -a -um	his/her/their (own)
syllaba -ae *f*	syllable

T

tabella -ae *f*	writing-tablet
tabellārius -ī *m*	letter-carrier
taberna -ae *f*	shop, stall
tabernārius -ī *m*	shopkeeper
tabula -ae *f*	writing-tablet
tacēre	be silent
tacitus -a -um	silent
talentum -ī *n*	talent
tālis -e	such
tam	so, as
tam-diū	so long, as long
tamen	nevertheless, yet
tam-quam	as, like
tandem	at length, at last
tangere tetigisse tāctum	touch
tantum -ī *n*	so much
alterum tantum	twice as much
tantum *adv*	so much, only
tantun-dem	just as much
tantus -a -um	so big, so great
tardus -a -um	slow, late
tata -ae *m*	daddy
taurus -ī *m*	bull
tēctum -ī *n*	roof
temerārius -a -um	reckless
tempestās -ātis *f*	storm
templum -ī *n*	temple
tempus -oris *n*	time
tenebrae -ārum *f pl*	darkness
tenebricōsus -a -um	dark
tenēre -uisse -ntum	hold, keep (back)
tenuis -e	thin
ter	three times
tergēre -sisse -sum	wipe
tergum -ī *n*	back
ternī -ae -a	three (each)
terra -ae *f*	earth, ground, country
terrēre	frighten
terribilis -e	terrible
tertius -a -um	third
testis -is *m/f*	witness
theātrum -ī *n*	theater
tībiae -ārum *f pl*	flute
tībīcen -inis *m*	flute-player
timēre	fear, be afraid (of)
timidus -a -um	fearful, timid
timor -ōris *m*	fear
titulus -ī *m*	title
toga -ae *f*	toga
togātus -a -um	wearing the toga
tollere sus-tulisse sublātum	raise, lift, pick up, remove, take away
tonitrus -ūs *m*	thunder
tot *indēcl*	so many
totiēs	so many times
tōtus -a -um	the whole of, all
trā-dere -didisse -ditum	hand over, deliver
trahere -āxisse -actum	drag, pull
tranquillitās -ātis *f*	calmness
tranquillus -a -um	calm, still
trāns *prp +acc*	across, over
trāns-ferre	transfer, transport
trāns-īre -eō -iisse -itum	cross, pass
tre-centī -ae -a	three hundred
trē-decim	thirteen
tremere -uisse	tremble
trēs tria	three
trīcēsimus -a -um	thirtieth
trīclīnium -ī *n*	dining-room
trīgintā	thirty
trīnī -ae -a	three
trīstis -e	sad
trīstitia -ae *f*	sadness
tū tē tibi	you, yourself
tuērī tūtum	guard, protect
tum	then
tumultuārī	make an uproar
tumultus -ūs *m*	uproar
tunc	then
tunica -ae *f*	tunic
turba -ae *f*	throng, crowd
turbāre	stir up, agitate
turbidus -a -um	agitated, stormy
turgid(ul)us -a -um	swollen
turpis -e	ugly, foul
tūtus -a -um	safe
tuus -a -um	your, yours
tyrannus -ī *m*	tyrant

U

ubi where
  ubi prīmum *+perf* as soon as
ubī-que everywhere
ūllus -a -um any
  nec/neque ūllus and no
ulterior -ius *comp* farther, more distant
ultimus -a -um *sup* most distant, last
ultrā *prp +acc* beyond
ululāre howl
umbra -a *f* shade, shadow
umerus -ī *m* shoulder
ūmidus -a -um wet, moist
umquam ever
  nec/neque umquam and never
ūnā *adv* together
unde from where
ūn-dē-centum ninety-nine
ūn-decim eleven
ūndecimus -a -um eleventh
ūn-dē-trīgintā twenty-nine
ūn-dē-vīgintī nineteen
ūnī -ae -a one
ūniversus -a -um the whole of, entire
ūnus -a -um one, only
urbānus -a -um of the city, urban
urbs -bis *f* city
ūrere ussisse ustum burn
ūsque up (to), all the time
ut like, as
  ut + *coni* that, in order that, to
uter utra utrum which (of the two)
uter-que utra- utrum- each of the two, both
ūtī ūsum *+abl* use, enjoy
utinam I wish that, if only…!
utrum…an …or…? whether…or
ūva -ae *f* grape
uxor -ōris *f* wife

V

vacuus -a -um empty
vāgīre wail, squall
valdē strongly, very (much)
valē -ēte farewell, goodbye
valēre be strong, be well
valētūdō -inis *f* health
validus -a -um strong
vallis -is *f* valley
vāllum -ī *n* rampart
varius -a -um varied, different
vās vāsis *n, pl* -a -ōrum vessel, bowl
-ve or
vehere vēxisse vectum carry, convey, *pass* ride, sail, travel
vel or
velle volō voluisse want, be willing
vēlōx -ōcis *adi* swift, rapid
vēlum -ī *n* sail
vel-ut like, as
vēna -ae *f* vein
vēn-dere -didisse sell
venīre vēnisse ventum come
venter -tris *m* belly, stomach
ventus -ī *m* wind
venustus -a -um charming
vēr vēris *n* spring
verbera -um *n pl* lashes, flogging
verberāre beat, flog
verbum -ī *n* word, verb
verērī fear
vērō really, however, but
  neque/nec vērō but not
versārī move about, be present
versiculus -ī *m* short verse
versus -ūs *m* line, verse
versus: ad…versus toward
vertere -tisse -sum turn
vērum but
vērus -a -um true, *n* truth
vesper -erī *m* evening
vesperī *adv* in the evening
vester -tra -trum your, yours
vestīgium -ī *n* footprint, trace
vestīmentum -ī *n* garment, clothing
vestīre dress
vestis -is *f* clothes, cloth
vestrum *gen* of you
vetāre forbid
vetus -eris *adi* old
via -ae *f* road, way, street
vīcēsimus -a -um twentieth
victor -ōris *m, adi* conqueror, victorious
victōria -ae *f* victory
vidēre vīdisse vīsum see, *pass* seem
vigilāre be awake
vigilia -ae *f* night watch (I-IV)
vīgintī twenty
vīlis -e cheap
vīlla -ae *f* country house, villa
vincere vīcisse victum defeat, overcome, win
vincīre -nxisse -nctum tie
vīnea -ae *f* vinyard
vīnum -ī *n* wine
vir -ī *m* man, husband
vīrēs -ium *f pl* strength
virga -ae *f* rod
virgō -inis *f* maiden, young girl
virtūs -ūtis *f* valor, courage
vīs, *acc* vim, *abl* vī force, violence, power
viscera -um *n pl* internal organs
vīsere -sisse go and see, visit
vīta -ae *f* life

vītāre	avoid
vītis -is *f*	vine
vīvere vīxisse	live, be alive
vīvus -a -um	living, alive
vix	hardly
vocābulum -ī *n*	word
vōcālis -is *f*	vowel
vocāre	call, invite
volāre	fly
voluntās -ātis *f*	will
vorāgō -inis *f*	abyss, whirlpool
vorāre	swallow, devour
vōs vōbīs	you, yourselves
vōx vōcis *f*	voice
vulnerāre	wound
vulnus -eris *n*	wound
vultus -ūs *m*	countenance, face

Z

zephyrus -ī *m*	west wind

GRAMMATICAL TERMS

LATIN	ABBREVIATIONS	ENGLISH
ablātīvus (cāsus)	*abl*	ablative
accūsātīvus (cāsus)	*acc*	accusative
āctīvum (genus)	*āct*	active
adiectīvum (nōmen)	*adi*	adjective
adverbium -ī *n*	*adv*	adverb
appellātīvum (nōmen)		appellative
cāsus -ūs *m*		case
comparātiō -ōnis *f*		comparison
comparātīvus (gradus)	*comp*	comparative
coniugātiō -ōnis *f*		conjugation
coniūnctiō -ōnis *f*	*coni*	conjunction
coniūnctīvus (modus)	*coni*	subjunctive
datīvus (cāsus)	*dat*	dative
dēclīnātiō -ōnis *f*	*dēcl*	declension
dēmōnstrātīvum (prōnōmen)		demonstrative
dēpōnentia (verba)	*dēp*	deponent
fēminīnum (genus)	*f, fēm*	feminine
futūrum (tempus)	*fut*	future
futūrum perfectum (tempus)	*fut perf*	future perfect
genetīvus (cāsus)	*gen*	genitive
genus (nōminis/verbī)		gender/voice
gerundium -ī *n*/ **gerundīvum** -ī *n*		gerund/gerundive
imperātīvus (modus)	*imp, imper*	imperative
imperfectum (tempus praeteritum)	*imperf*	imperfect
indēclīnābile (vocābulum)	*indēcl*	indeclinable
indēfīnītum (prōnōmen)		indefinite
indicātīvus (modus)	*ind*	indicative
īnfīnītīvus (modus)	*īnf*	infinitive
interiectiō -ōnis *f*		interjection
interrogātīvum (prōnōmen)		interrogative
locātīvus (cāsus)	*loc*	locative
masculīnum (genus)	*m, masc*	masculine
modus (verbī)		mode
neutrum (genus)	*n, neutr*	neuter
nōminātīvus (cāsus)	*nōm*	nominative
optātīvus (modus)		optative
pars ōrātiōnis		part of speech
participium -ī *n*	*part*	participle
passīvum (genus)	*pass*	passive
perfectum (tempus praeteritum)	*perf*	perfect
persōna -ae *f*	*pers*	person
persōnāle (prōnōmen)		personal
plūrālis (numerus)	*pl, plūr*	plural
plūsquamperfectum (tempus praet.)	*plūsqu*	pluperfect
positīvus (gradus)	*pos*	positive
possessīvum (prōnōmen)		possessive
praepositiō -ōnis *f*	*prp, praep*	preposition
praesēns (tempus)	*praes*	present
praeteritum (tempus)	*praet*	preterite, past tense
prōnōmen -inis *n*	*prōn*	pronoun
proprium (nōmen)		proper name
relātīvum (prōnōmen)	*rel*	relative
singulāris (numerus)	*sg, sing*	singular
superlātīvus (gradus)	*sup*	superlative
supīnum		supine
tempus (verbī)		tense
verbum	*vb*	verb
vocātīvus (cāsus)	*voc*	vocative